SELL YOURSELF WITHOUT SAYING A WORD

The Experts' Guide
to Placing Articles
In Print and Online

RUSSELL TRAHAN

INDIE BOOKS
INTERNATIONAL

ISBN-10: 1-941870-97-X
ISBN-13: 978-1-941870-97-6
Library of Congress Control Number: 2017944866

Designed by Joni McPherson, mcphersongraphics.com

INDIE BOOKS INTERNATIONAL, LLC
2424 VISTA WAY, SUITE 316
OCEANSIDE, CA 92054

www.indiebooksintl.com

CONTENTS

PREFACE

Publicity 101 is knowing who your target market is. Publicity 102 is knowing where your target market is. Regardless of whether your target market is stay-at-home parents with young children and aging parents, or entrepreneurs who built their businesses up to mid-sized regional powerhouses, there is a magazine they're reading in print or online. You can get your expertise in front of them by placing articles in those magazines.

Russell Trahan
President, PR/PR Public Relations
April, 2017

"It's a how-to article about how to write how-to articles."

Why Write an Article?

As an expert, one of the fastest ways to get your content, your unique position, your controversial stance in front of your target audience is through article placements. It doesn't matter if you are a wine expert, a management consultant, or biblically-based financial planner, there is a magazine, newsletter, e-zine, or some form of communication, either in print or online, aimed at your target market.

For the sake of this book, the examples used will be for professional speakers, consultants, or nonfiction authors simply because those are the niche markets served by my company, PR/PR Public Relations. Our media relations lie in the trade, industry, and business association publications situated to benefit experts looking for name recognition in front of business decision makers looking to hire for conventions, conferences, and corporate events.

For the wine expert, there are local neighborhood magazines around your shop; for the biblically-based financial planner there are magazines and websites targeted towards single parents and seniors. There are magazines for women and parenting, there are magazines for men's interests; there is a magazine for any subject you can think of—especially online.

Just because you are not a management consultant or sales trainer, don't think you won't benefit from the principles in this book—you will! The principles are the same, just change the topic/title/website of the publications I reference into the ones relating to your expertise.

The Power of Industry and Association Publications

Studies have shown that business owners, executives, entrepreneurs, and C-suite-level decision makers read their industry publications and association magazines cover-to-cover every month—more often than they read an entire edition of the *The Wall Street Journal* or an entire issue of *Entrepreneur*.

Plus, in a trade, industry, or business association publication you are more likely to get an entire article of your content placed, with a bio paragraph at the end. Newsstand magazines and daily newspapers use writers, reporters, freelancers, and columnists who will quote you as an expert, but rarely take unsolicited articles from outside sources.

Many speakers and consultants think they'll achieve instant fame and build their career if only they were quoted in a major magazine or daily newspaper, such as *USA Today*. While that would be great, and sounds fantastic when being introduced at the podium, what will most likely get you invited to that podium in the first place is an article placed directly in front of meeting planners in their association publication.

After all, to reach your target market from a quote in *USA Today*, you have to hope that your target is staying in a hotel (because that's where most people read *USA Today*), and you have to hope that they don't just step over that day's edition on their way out the door. If they finally decide to thumb through the paper you have to hope they read the section you're quoted in, the article you're quoted in, and you have to hope that they read down to the paragraph you're quoted in. Those are too many variables.

The same can be said for high-profile online outlets, such as *HuffPost*. You have to hope your target market checks the website on the day your article is posted. You have to hope they go to the category where your article is posted. You have to hope you're still at the top of the page, or that they scroll down far enough to find your article. Once again, too many variables.

Experts of all kinds often seek the "celebrity" status of TV or radio. While this works to feed the ego, it does not help build your business. There's a phrase in the broadcast industry called, "ten and done!" This means that if a viewer or listener does not respond to your message within ten minutes of hearing it, chances are they never will. How often have you, yourself, been listening to the radio, hear a great author or expert giving advice, but by the time you've gotten home or to the office, you've been hit with hundreds of other messages and have forgotten the name of the book and the expert?

When your expertise—in the form of an article—is in print or online, the reader can save the magazines, tear out the page, bookmark the URL, download a copy, or e-mail a link to a friend. This gives them the ability to react to your message the next week, the next month, or even the next year. Think of the executive who reads an article in the August issue of his trade magazine, likes the advice given and decides to give copies of the author's book to his staff for Christmas. We hear all the time from meeting planners that they look to their industry and association publications for speakers for their next event. If your expertise is deemed applicable to their readership, you'll be a safe speaker for their audience.

Articles Generate Credibility

This flows right into the instant credibility, the stamp of endorsement, that being in a magazine provides you. Whether you've been speaking for two years or twenty, when you're in a trade or association publication, you're the expert on the subject. The reader doesn't care how long you've been giving keynotes and workshops. All they care about is how you can make their lives and businesses better.

You'll read in the subsequent chapter on pitching your article that the editor doesn't care, either. With all the online placements these days, it will give your website a jump in search engine optimization (SEO) that can't be beat. Your URL can quickly outrank that of a well-established speaker with all the trade and industry sites that post your article and link back to your site from theirs.

> Article placements give you a "warm call" or an open door to reach out to the associations that have placed your content and market yourself for speaking engagements.

You'll read in an upcoming chapter about marketing with an article, and that whether the placement is in a direct association publication or a wider-reaching trade or industry publication you'll have multiple avenues to open new business opportunities.

©Glasbergen
glasbergen.com

GLASBERGEN

"Look, I want honest feedback about my article before you
submit. Do you love it, or do you really love it?"

How to Write an Article

Now that you know why you should write articles, let's talk about how to write them.

Article writing is unlike any other form of writing, such as blogging or book writing, though both are good sources for article topics.

The topic is the first step in article writing. Most people think it's the title, but it is much easier to drape the content of the article around a topic than it is to try to force the content underneath a title. Once you have written the article, a pithy, benefit-oriented title usually floats out of the content, so start with the topic.

When It Pays to be Non-Specific

Topics should be evergreen. Don't pin your article down to a specific current event or time of year. If you want to write about football, don't write about the Super Bowl because editors will only use it in January and/or February. If you want to write about a holiday, don't write about Independence Day because editors will only use it in July. Rather, write about non-specific football games or holidays in general, so editors can place your article when they would like.

The exception is current events with historic significance, and using them in historical context. When a client wanted to reference the Exxon Valdez in April of 1989, just a few weeks after the oil spill, I suggested against it because once the disaster was cleaned up and the media moved on to the next natural disaster the article would not get much placement. However, referencing the incident today, as a business and/or natural disaster, would give the reader a common experience to relate to with the author.

As I said above, blogs and books make excellent article topics. Did you have a blog that was particularly popular? You could easily change the tense of the blog from first-person to second-person, and, probably, lengthen it to the 800 to 1,000 words that editors prefer. Books are great because each of the chapters in your book can simply become a bulleted section in the article, boiling them down to seventy-five to 100 words and then choosing the five to seven that best go together, giving the reader an overview of your book. From there, you can take a chapter you made into a bulleted section and expand it out to a full article for your next offering, creating a series of articles.

For Future Articles Look to the Past

Another great source for article topics is past articles. If you have a particularly popular article, you can always take one of the bulleted sections from it and expand on that content so that it forms an 800- to 1,000-word-piece, adding new bulleted sections underneath the new introduction. For example, in sample articles you will find later in this book, the one titled "Talent vs. Determination" by Walt Grassl did so well (more than twenty placements), we later pulled out the "Life Long Learning" section of that article and expanded it into its own article, which did equally as well.

Editors also love articles that feature lists and acronyms. Lists can be along the lines of:

- Top Five Things You Can Do To Improve…

- Seven Ways To…

- Six Mistakes You Didn't Know…

Acronyms are wonderful as well. In Patricia Fripp's article "ROCK Star Communication", the acronym is R = Rehearse, O = Opening, C = Core Message, and K = Kick A$$ Closing.

The Secrets of Structure

Once you have a topic established, it's time

to structure and format the article. As I said above, these days editors prefer articles that are between 800 and 1,000 words. Some may want shorter, and you should allow them to edit your article for their space allotment—just make sure they keep your contact information intact. Other editors may want you to elaborate on your ideas and expand your article into a full feature for them. Depending on who their readership is—and how much work the editor is asking for—the call is yours to do this or not.

No I, We, or Me

Don't write your article in first person. Writing in first person will be seen as too advertorial and too self-promotional to the editors and they won't run your article; instead, they'll want you to buy an ad. When you write in second person the readers are more likely to identify themselves in the article, agree with your premise, and take the action step at the end you'd like them to.

> Don't quote other experts or authors. The whole point of the article is to set up you, the author, as the expert.

If you quote another author, why would the readers buy your book? They'll just buy the other author's book. If you quote another speaker, why would the readers hire you for their next convention when they can just hire that speaker? The exception to this rule is historical figures. It's all right to quote Benjamin Franklin—nobody will be hiring him to keynote their next convention.

Do start with an introductory paragraph. This should be about 100 words and introduces the situation, problem, or scenario the article is based on. You can open with a story, you can open with a statistic, you can open with a quote. There are many ways to tell the readers what they're going to read about, as long as it's to the point and not misleading.

The second paragraph is where you draw the reader in, relating the opening to them, using the second person tense. "You may be having this problem…," "You could be feeling this way…," "Does this happen in your business?" are just some examples of how to do this. There are hundreds, so use the one that works best for readership.

From there you get into your bulleted sections. These don't have to literally be bullet points; they can be numbered, or lettered, or key-word delineated paragraphs, each one giving your reader an action step, or solution, or benefit related to the topic of the article. In this post-MTV world, this gives the reader the opportunity to pick up your article, put it down, then pick it back up again and get a benefit from your expertise each time. The length of each bulleted section depends on how many bulleted sections you want. Generally, this part of your article is about 800 words, so if you have four sections you can make each one 200 words, but if you're trying to get ten in you'll only have eighty words for each.

End with Punch

The conclusion is your wrap-up time. Let your readers know how wonderful and rosy their lives/businesses will be when they follow your advice. This is not the time to bring up new topics or issues. Most conclusions run fifty to 100 words. So keep them short, because the readers already have what they need from your article.

Following the conclusion is your resource box, or the About the Author paragraph. This is where all the promoting comes in. In this paragraph you will tell the readers exactly what you want them to know about you and what action step you want them to take. Be specific.

We had a client for years who touted themselves as consultants in their resource box. I knew from talking to their staff that they had received consulting business from the articles placements. When the owner called to end our agreement, however, she claimed it was because she had never received a single *speaking engagement* from the articles placements.

So, in the traditional fifty- to seventy-five-word limit for your resource box, be careful to say exactly what you want from the reader and give them the link to your website to get it. It may be tempting, but don't go too long on the resource paragraph. Editors will cut them, and they may cut what you think is the most important part. The closer you can stay to fifty words—including your website address at the end—the more likely you'll be to get the whole paragraph included.

"I just read your trade journal article. I don't know you, but
I must have you in my life."

CHAPTER 3

Where to Pitch an Article

N ow that you know how to write an article, let's talk about where to pitch it out.

Pitch is the keyword here. You don't want to simply blast out the article, allowing it to be placed anywhere and everywhere, with outlets that may not properly evaluate the content they use. You want to pitch your article directly to your target audience, regardless of the size of the circulation or views.

If your target market reads a publication cover-to-cover every month, it doesn't matter if it only has a circulation of 500 if it means that 100 percent of them can hire you. This contrasts with your article being placed on websites with potentially larger readerships, but its audiences don't apply to your target market.

You should be wary of online article depositories. These are often unregulated, with no way of tracking by whom and how often your articles are read or copied elsewhere.

At PR/PR we only use one online article depository, *Article Weekly*, to post our clients' articles. It is editorially controlled by Peter DeHaan, who is also a magazine editor. He reviews each article for quality of content prior to posting, and is always great about including the author's contact information. We've had several calls from people who have read our clients' articles on *Article Weekly* and wanted to reprint them in their training material or handbooks, to which, of course, we grant permission, as long as the contact information remains intact.

Learn What Your Audience Reads

Pitching out the article is going to take a little bit of research. This shouldn't be a terribly involved process, thanks to Google. Know what audience you want to be in front of, know what they read, and confirm that the publication takes unsolicited articles from outside sources.

Let's say you want to be in front of real estate brokers. You know that they are reading their real estate association magazine, newsletter, and/or e-zine. These are published/posted at the local, regional, and national levels. With a little bit of searching you can find the state, regional, and national realtors associations. From their websites you can identify the methods that they use to communicate with their members, who edits them, and if they accept article submissions. Now the pitching can begin.

You'll want to tease out the article, not merely send out the entire text.

> Highlight the benefit of your content to that editor's readership, offering them the full text of the article in exchange for running your contact information with it.

Be sure—always, every time, without exception—to let the editor know that you are offering the article *for free on a non-exclusive basis*. This is how you can get the same article placed multiple times, across multiple industries, all over the country.

Pitch the Article with a Press Release

Please review the following sample press release.

FOR IMMEDIATE RELEASE

The Most Desired Skills of the Future

*Free Article for your publication by Nathan Jamail

How many parents have a toddler that can work an iPhone or iPad better than they can? What about the parents of teenage kids or young adults that cannot communicate except through texting, e-mail or social media? With technology constantly evolving, technical skills and know-how will be the most common skills among the working and business public—but the ability to communicate face to face will always be one of the most important aspects of business.

While younger generations preparing to enter the workforce should keep up with technology to remain relevant in today's economy, they should also continue to practice and focus on perfecting their soft skills—communication, interpersonal interaction, influence and personal effectiveness in a social and business setting. These abilities are the great *differentiator* in business of the future.

In his latest article, "The Most Desired Skills of the Future," sales coach Nathan Jamail provides your readers with the top three techniques managers can employ to cultivate these skills in their staff, which are:

- Coaching, not managing

- Implementing a practice program

- Focusing on coaching soft skills

Nathan Jamail, best-selling author of "The Playbook Series," is also a motivational speaker, entrepreneur and corporate coach. As a former executive for Fortune 500 companies, and owner of several small businesses, Nathan travels the country helping individuals and organizations achieve maximum success. A few of his clients include Fidelity, Nationwide Insurance, The Hartford Group, Cisco, Stryker Communications, and Army National Guard.

This article is being offered to your publication free of charge on a non-exclusive basis. We ask in return that you print the author's resource box and contact information. We also ask that you send two copies of the issue in which the article appears. If you decide to use the article online or in an e-newsletter, please hyperlink to the author's website and send us a link or PDF file.

To obtain a copy of this article or to interview Nathan, please contact:

Carter Breazeale
PR/PR Public Relations
407-895-8800
CommAgent@prpr.net

# # #

Now let's break it down piece by piece.

The opening paragraph(s) basically mirrors the introductory paragraph from the article, setting up the situation or problem the article is going to solve. The next paragraph is used to relate the solutions to the reader, briefly introducing the author with his or her key credentials.

It isn't until at least the third paragraph that you give the bio of the author. This is intentional. All editors care about is the content of the article and how well it's written and edited. As long as the content relates to their association and benefits their readership, they don't care if the author went to Harvard or Wossamotta U. End the press release with the contact information necessary for the editor to obtain a copy of the article and/or interview the author. Some publications prefer to run exclusive content, in which case, they may counter your article pitch with an interview opportunity. This allows them to run an exclusive, and you still receive a placement in front of your target market.

But When Will the Article Appear?

After you've sent the editor the full text of the article, it gives you the opportunity to follow up with the editor on the placement status of your content. We usually give them a couple of weeks to read it over and decide if/when they'll be publishing or posting the article.

Now, you've already indicated in the initial pitch that you would like to receive print copies or link proofs once your piece has been used, and you've asked them the same when they requested the complete text, but this doesn't necessarily mean that the editor will follow through. Most are really good about returning the favor of your giving them quality content by dropping the issue in which it appeared into the mail, but others will take persistent follow up.

Of course, you're going to set up a Google Alert to catch most online placements, but for the editors who change the title (and some will, which is all right as long as your contact information remains intact) you'll need to go back to them and ask if/when they'll be placing it.

Some editors will take the full text and place it on their website the next day or in an e-zine the next week. Some editors will take the full text and want to place it in their next issue, but they work sixty to ninety days out, so you'll have to wait eight to twelve weeks to see the print issue. Other editors may take the full text and want to place it in a special themed issue they have coming out six months, or more, from the initial request. This is when you'll need to mark your calendar to circle back with the editor and ask again for that link and/or print version.

We pitch one article every six to eight weeks. This formula has been honed over nearly twenty years of placing articles. In the arena of articles placement, quantity of articles does not equate to quality results. If you approach an editor with one, two, or three articles at a time, there's a high probability of only one being selected for placement, and the others rejected outright. From a pitching perspective, this then erases your opportunity to individually pitch those articles in the future. However, if you go to the editor every eight weeks, you have a better chance of getting all three articles placed in subsequent issues.

Also, if you go to editors too often, they may have previously said they like article A and will place it in their next issue which is sixty to ninety days out, so if you go back to them a couple of weeks later with article B, they may like B better and slide it into the slot reserved for A, and you only get one article placed, not both of them. Getting multiple articles placed in multiple issues gives you the frequency and repetition necessary for a great publicity campaign. By pitching out multiple articles at the same time, you essentially burn two articles which may have generated immense traction on their own.

©Glasbergen
glasbergen.com

GLASBERGEN

"I laughed, I cried, it became a part of me. We must hire the author of this article as our next 401K consultant."

When to Market from an Article

Now that you know how to get an article placed, let's talk about what to do with the publicity you'll be getting.

There are many ways you can use the publicity you're getting from the placements while you build the name recognition through frequency and repetition of placements. Let's start online.

Since each of your online placements will feature a link back to your website, it's important that you return the favor by linking from your website back to the placement. Search-engine algorithms love reciprocal links. Don't worry about getting multiple placements of the same article online; if the other sites are posting your article to their site it does not affect your search rankings like it does if you posted the same article to multiple sites.

Capitalize on the Placement

After you've received several online placements for your article you can add an "In the Media" or "As Seen In" page or tab to your website. You can post the introduction to the article, or a summary of the benefits (like you used to pitch it out), on this page, then put links to the placements underneath it. You can use an image of the magazine cover, or the logo of the magazine, or just the link; this is not as important as just making sure the link is there.

After you've pitched out several articles and had several placements of each, you can reorganize your webpage by industry; such as: "These retailers like these articles:" or "These manufacturers like these articles." This will show meeting planners in one quick glance that you're an expert in their field.

It should go without saying, but I'll say it anyway: utilize the online placements that you receive on your social media platforms. Focus on LinkedIn, but also use Twitter and your Facebook business page. It's easy to post all these from Hootsuite, or whatever scheduling tool you prefer. Don't be too verbose when you post, just a simple comment of thanks to the publication for using your content and a link to the article. You want to self-promote, not be braggadocious.

Be sure to use the placements—either logos of the magazines or images of the cover of the issue you're in—in your marketing materials. Whether it's your one-sheet, your mailers, or any printed collateral you send out, don't be shy about using them with existing clients as well. It will remind any meeting planners you're already working with that you are the recognized expert and you are in demand.

Enter the Meeting Planner

Once you're ready to start marketing yourself

to associations from your article placements you'll need to identify the contact information for the meeting planner, marketing director, or chief-paid-officer of the association, whomever is in charge of booking the speakers. The editor you've built the relationship with to get the article placed is not the right person to reach out to about speaking at the association's event. Fortunately, finding the meeting planner is very easy on associations' websites these days.

Some of the placements you'll get might be directly in association publications. You'll be able to go to their website, find when their upcoming meetings and events are, and who the meeting planner is in just a couple of clicks. These are the easy ones. The placements you get in trade or industry publications will take a little more research, but they also offer greater options for marketing. If you get into an insurance industry publication, you can easily search for any and all insurance publications, go to their websites, identify the contact information for meeting planners and the upcoming meetings and events on their calendar. You'll be able to contact half a dozen or more associations from just one placement!

When you do identify an association to contact from a placement of your article, look at the chapters at the local, regional, and national levels. They all have meetings and they all have budgets for speakers. Your local chapter would be particularly interested in booking you from your article placement to save them money on travel expenses. If there is an event in your town by an association with whom you've secured a placement—even if they've already booked the speakers—let them know you're available in case someone already contracted drops out or has to cancel. Being local, you'll be the first one they'll call to fill the gap in their program.

Look at sister associations affiliated with the placements you receive. If you get an article placed in a bar association publication, you could use that to market yourself to the judicial associations and law enforcement associations, as well as the legal association you've already been in front of. The same is true for a real estate association respecting a placement you've had in an insurance or financial planning association publication.

A Final Thought

The frequency and repetition of publicity that article placements give you will help you stand out above the competition.

Picture, if you will, a meeting planner deciding on who will keynote at next year's annual convention. He's gathered up one-sheets and demo DVDs from speakers bureaus and previous speakers. He has them scattered all about the conference room table, essentially saying to himself, "Eenie meenie miney mo, who should stay and who should go?" When your content is in a meeting planner's trade magazine or industry publication, that meeting planner will say out loud, "Eenie meenie miney, oh! *This* is the speaker I've got to hire!"

42

"This article says we're not placing enough emphasis on diversity."

APPENDIX A

Sample Articles

Editor's Note: The following seven articles are not edited to the *Chicago Manual of Style*, which is the style bible for the publishing industry. These articles are edited to the *Associated Press Stylebook and Libel Manual*, which is the style bible for the magazine and newspaper world.

▶ SAMPLE ARTICLE ONE

This article was abridged from Patricia Fripp's e-Book, Rock Star Communications: How to Inspire Action and Commitment. *When she first sent me the e-Book my initial instinct was to pick five to seven of the seventeen "secrets" Patricia had written, but as I read the e-Book, I was struck by the inspiration that we could alter the article from an "X Secrets of…" style to the acronym article you see below. At PR/PR we often take article topics from other mediums (blogs, books, etc.), but sometimes we even take existing content and format it in an entirely different fashion.*

ROCK Star Communication

How to Inspire Action and Commitment

by Patricia Fripp

In an era of tough competition, presentations that persuade, educate, motivate, and inspire give you a competitive edge. Good presentation skills are no longer simply nice to have; they can mean career life or death.

Imagine yourself in the front row of a ballroom at a convention. Sitting with you are sales professionals from all over the world. This was a software company's challenging January sales meeting.

That company had recently bought a competitor, and 40% of the sales professionals had nothing to do with the decision.

The opening speaker, the company's president, was challenged with getting everyone to know that they are working for the right company at the right time, that the company's strategy is sound, and that working for them will prove beneficial toward their career. He is an engineer, a brilliant leader, and rather shy. He is not a bad speaker; for this meeting, however, he knows he needs to become the corporate *Rock Star*.

Here are the Rock Star Principles that our shy engineer used and that you can also use to become a Rock Star communicator in the business world.

Rock Star Principle 1: R = Rehearse

Great performers and rock stars value rehearsal.

When your message is internalized, you know your structure, could wake up in the middle of the night and deliver your opening and closing, and have informally told your stories, get serious about rehearsal and delivery.

When you walk on stage, stand still at front center while you deliver your opening remarks.

When you move, do not wander aimlessly; it makes you look nervous!

Before an important presentation, schedule daily rehearsal. Rehearse in your own environment. Then rehearse on the stage where you will be speaking.

You need to know how many steps it takes to get to the center of the stage. Work with the production company and the audiovisual technicians. Their job is to make you look good. They can't do their job as effectively if you do not take your sound checks and rehearsals seriously. If possible, do this the day before.

Rock Star Principle 2: O = Opening

The first 30 to 60 seconds of your speech set the tone. They help build anticipation.

"Good morning, ladies and gentlemen. What a pleasure to be here." Sounds polite, but it is predictable, boring, and will not inspire action or commitment. It is not Rock Star quality. Rock Star performers will tell you, "We open with our second best song and close with our best." These performers may have conversation with the audience to thank them for attending or for years of support but not at the opening!

You may be thinking, "I have 45 minutes for my speech. That's plenty of time to warm up and connect." Wrong. Your audience is full of stimulation junkies with short attention spans. Come out punching, and grab the audience's attention. Make them think, "Wow! This is going to be good!"

An audience will forgive you for anything except being boring. Predictability is boring.

Start with a story, dramatic statement, question, or an inspiring thought. The software president walked out and said, "Welcome to a brand new company!" He then described what had happened that made this the best move ever.

Rock Star Principle 3: C = Core Message

Each rock tour has a theme.

Know your central theme and core message. Your opening remarks must logically transition into the main message. The body will prove your central idea.

After his opening line, the executive answered the audience's unspoken questions: why was the decision made, what would it mean to them, and why was he the best leader?

The *person behind the position* is the person they would fight for, work long hours for, and whose corporate strategy gives them confidence. We respect the position; we get emotionally connected to the person.

It is not only what you say that communicates your message. It is also the subtext, what you aren't saying outright.

Rock Star communicators also realize that in order to inspire action, you need to appeal to the audience's rational self-interest. People make decisions for their reasons, not yours. They need to understand what is in it for them.

Rock Star Principle 4: K = Kick-A$$ Closing

Remember, rock stars always close on their best song. Review your key ideas, and you have many options to close on a high.

Close your presentation with the same words, thought, or vision from your opening. Remember, your last words linger. Leave them with a reinforcement of a key idea or an inspirational thought from your presentation. Consider the technique that the software president used.

If you are going to be a Rock Star presenter who inspires action and commitment, do not compete with yourself! Your audience can't listen and read. A boring PowerPoint with too many words or too much information can sabotage a great presentation. Did your audience come to read or to hear you?

Good luck with your journey to inspire action and commitment as a Rock Star communicator.

Even though you were not sitting in the front row of a ballroom at a convention, you now have powerhouse suggestions for becoming a Rock Star communicator yourself.

About the Author

 Patricia Fripp is an executive speech coach, sales presentation skills trainer, on-line training expert and subject matter expert for Continuing Education at XTRACredits. Her brother, Robert Fripp, is a Rock Star and legendary guitarist with King Crimson. When your message must be memorable in-person or online Patricia Fripp can help. To become a great speaker easily, conveniently and quickly sign up for a trial at FrippVT.com.

▶ SAMPLE ARTICLE TWO

This article went gangbusters, being placed in nearly twenty print and online trade, industry, and association publications. It proved that editors loved the material, and would want more of it, so we went back to the client and discussed the idea of taking one of the bulleted sections and expanding it into its own article. The "Willingness to Learn" section was a favorite of the client's, so we decided to form a feature article out of it. When an article does particularly well, we often utilize its content to form topics for entirely new articles.

Talent versus Determination

By Walt Grassl

Bob and Mark are new managers who are having lunch in the company cafeteria. They are discussing their respective hiring strategies for the upcoming college job fair that their company is sponsoring. The conversation turned into a debate on what type of graduate made the best employee.

Mark prefers to hire the 4.0 GPA graduates, regardless of how driven they appear or how well they seem to "play with others." He figures he could instill the drive and the teamwork.

Bob believes in hiring smart, but not necessarily the smartest (3.0 and above GPAs) and wanted those who demonstrate determination and good collaboration skills. He figures they are smart enough to learn and their drive and teamwork would carry the day.

Patricia, a seasoned manager, joined in the discussion and shared her thoughts about the importance of hard work and talent in the workforce. She believes that if people don't have a minimum amount of talent, hard work may not be enough for them to be successful. Conversely, some of the most talented people aren't successful in their careers because they don't work hard. The most successful people have talent and they work hard.

Patricia is right. Hard-working, talented people make the best employees. As an employee, we must consider what is in our control and what can we influence. We cannot control how much talent we have. But we can control how hard we work and how hard we persevere when times get tough.

Here are five character traits for hiring managers to consider.

Reaction to praise

Studies have shown that when people are praised for their intelligence, they tend to avoid risk when given a choice their next assignments. Why? If they are less than perfect in the future, they are afraid of not looking as smart. However, when people are praised for their hard work in completing their assignment, they welcome more challenging assignments. If they work hard on a task that their leadership recognizes has a high degree of difficulty and they come up short, they have a history that indicates their hard work will be acknowledged.

Ability to adapt to change

In the workplace, success often depends upon the ability to change from one process to another. Often times, highly talented people have a set way of doing things and it works extremely well for them. They do not like to change what worked in the past and made them the success that they are. Change requires hard work, and while many talented people do well adapting to change, some who feel that they have extraordinary talent are not so flexible.

Willingness to learn

Many talented people feel that they do not have

anything new to learn in their chosen field. They believe what got them there is enough.

Those who are determined and who work hard, often spend a lot of time and effort to maintain their skills and learn new skills. They often display the most current knowledge of new technology and ideas. Having employees who will improve themselves over and above the company sponsored training is critical to an organization wanting to innovate and improve.

Different expectations

People who are highly talented may believe they are entitled to a certain pay level, promotional opportunities and respect. They can be the workplace equivalent of rockstars and elite athletes.

Those who succeed based on hard work over talent tend to have more realistic expectations.

Those who depend on demonstrating their work ethic and their determination to succeed often will find that their hard work pays off in terms of promotions, pay increases and the level of respect they earn in the workplace. Unlike their more talented co-workers, they tend to avoid resting on their laurels.

Not everyone who is talented depends entirely on their talent to find success in the workplace. Many of those with a great deal of talent work hard, often as hard as their less talented co-workers. However, in some cases, those who are highly talented often feel that they need not work as hard to get ahead. Nearly anyone who sets his or her mind to finding success can be successful; however without hard work, few will ever find a level of success that will pay off for them over time.

Goal Setting

People who set goals are usually more successful than those who don't. The best goals to set are "stretch" goals. Stretch goals are attainable and challenging, but realistic. If you set goals that are too easy, you will accomplish them more often but not be as satisfied. Satisfaction comes from pursuing a goal, not from ultimately achieving it.

Focus on one objective at a time and always have the next goal in mind. To accomplish more difficult tasks, break these down into smaller tasks. Try to have mini goals along the way and try to map out several different paths to your target: this allows flexibility if one path becomes blocked. Activity itself generates the impetus for further activity.

Determination and perseverance are important traits in the workplace. Employers want employees who are determined to get things done, to make things happen and to constantly look for better ways of doing things. **We are more likely to continue in the face of adversity if we think talent is only peripheral to our future success.** Persistence and purposeful effort are more important than talent.

Studies have observed that when facing difficulties, those who believed that their performance was transformable through effort, not only persevered but actually improved, whereas those who believed that talent was everything regressed.

Don't rely on your talents. Develop the practices of hard work, determination and perseverance, and you will be able to maximize your success.

About the Author

Walt Grassl is a speaker, author of "Stand Up and Speak Up," and host of the Internet radio show, "Stand Up and Speak Up." Walt's accomplishments include success in Toastmasters International speech contests and performing standup comedy at the Hollywood Improv and the Flamingo in Las Vegas. For more information on bringing Walt Grassl to your next event, please visit WaltGrassl.com.

▶ SAMPLE ARTICLE THREE

This is the article that came out of the author's previous article, "Talent v Determination." It also did well, placing above the fourteen average placements for a single article.

Education is Continuous
Five Pillars to Ensure You Never Stop Learning
By Walt Grassl

Many talented people feel that they do not have anything new to learn in their chosen field. They believe what got them there is enough.

Those who are determined and who work hard often spend a lot of time and effort to learn new skills and maintain their existing ones.

They display the most current knowledge of new technology and ideas. Having employees who will improve themselves over and above the company-sponsored training is critical to an organization wanting to innovate and improve.

Eleven years ago, Ben got a job working in the mail room at a local business during the summer before starting college. The company had been in existence for over sixty years and was currently being led by Jack—a long-time employee and company legend who started in the mailroom. Three weeks into the job, on his way from the basement to the top floor, the elevator stopped and who should enter the elevator but Jack. He smiled at Ben, introduced himself, and mentioned that he started out in the mail room. Ben was a little star struck, but as they both exited the elevator, Ben asked if Jack had any advice for him.

"Never stop educating yourself," Jack said. "In fact, come into my office and let me elaborate. I have 15 minutes before my next meeting."

Jack proceeded to share these five pillars for continued education:

1. You are responsible for your education

You alone are responsible for your education. Whether or not it makes sense to invest in a formal education, there are free and for-fee learning opportunities available to everyone. The public library and the Internet are two examples.

Another invaluable source of education is through people. Spend time with people who can do things that you can't. It may mean volunteering to stay late to observe someone, going to lunch with more experienced associates or finding a mentor.

You can also learn by taking on challenging assignments that are above your skill level. Discuss the help you will need to be successful and the company leadership may reward your initiative by providing an experienced staff member oversee your on-the-job training.

You can learn pretty much anything, if you work hard at it.

2. No entitlements

Time in service should be no guarantee of advancement in a successful business. It is what one learns with his or her experience that determines the value of the service time. In other words, if you put in your time, you are guaranteed nothing.

As your time with the company grows, seek lateral transfers or increased responsibility without necessarily a corresponding increase in title or pay. Realize you are making yourself more valuable to your employer and view the stretch assignments as an investment in yourself.

Although we are living in a time of an increasing sense of entitlement, we must all take care of ourselves.

3. You can't rest on your laurels

Many talented people feel that they do not have anything new to learn in their chosen field. They believe what got them there is enough. They become complacent. They decide they don't need to put in more effort and stop striving for success.

When you reach a goal, celebrate your success, but identify your next goal and begin to take action. When you stop moving forward and rest on your laurels, in actuality you are falling behind all the others who continue to move forward.

4. Staying current

Likewise, you need to stay current with industry trends by reading industry literature and blogs. If you are moving into management, read leadership books and blogs. New trends are frequently entering the workplace. You have the choice to be aware of and lead the change or try to catch up—or even worse—resisting the change.

Joining industry and trade associations is another way to educate yourself on current trends.

5. New and old generation

A big issue in many industries is getting several generations to work well together. Each generation has different learning and working styles. You have several options to handle this reality. The first is to do nothing, since it's your fellow employee's responsibility to get with the program. You can leave it to your company's leadership to implement a program to fix the problem. The higher percentage choice is to educate yourself on the differences between generations, the issues these differences bring to the workplace and some things others are doing to address them.

You can use this information to change how you interact and to the extent you can, help your company improve their processes.

Ben took Jack's advice to heart. After graduating from college, he got a job with another company in another field. His education did not stop when he left school.

He subscribes to industry and management blogs, has joined his industry association and seeks out challenging assignments and develops relationships with other successful employees at his company. He has been identified by his management as a high-potential employee and is one of the youngest employees at his level. Ben's future is bright. Amazing what a chance encounter in an elevator can do.

About the Author

 Walt Grassl is a speaker, author, and performer. He hosts the radio show, "Stand Up and Speak Up," on the RockStar Worldwide network. Walt has performed standup comedy at the Hollywood Improv and the Flamingo in Las Vegas and is studying improv at the Groundlings School in Hollywood. For more information on bringing Walt Grassl to your next event, please visit www.WaltGrassl.com.

▶ SAMPLE ARTICLE FOUR

This article is an example of how PR/PR Public Relations practices what it preaches. It was pitched out to trade, industry, and association publications, and received a dozen or more placements in print and online. The article was ghostwritten by PR/PR Agent Carter Breazeale. Many of PR/PR's clients use a ghostwriter. Either they don't have the time to write, or don't enjoy writing. As long as the work is in the client's voice, it doesn't matter who wrote it for them.

Media Mixology

Crafting the Perfect Publicity Cocktail

By Russell Trahan

The handcrafted cocktail has skyrocketed in popularity. Thanks in part to period-piece television dramas such as *Mad Men* that romanticize bar scenes of yore, drinks like the Old Fashioned and the Sazerac have risen from the recesses of the speakeasy to the drink menu of the neighborhood watering hole. With its focus on precision and detail, the art of mixology has effectively taken taps and brass rails by storm.

From the bar room to the board room, a different brand of mixology is taking place: the meticulously designed publicity campaign. All beneficial and lucrative PR strategies are devised like a classic cocktail, with an emphasis on industry-standards, creative execution and an array of unique approaches that parallel the goals—*or tastes*—of the business or individual. There are many different options to consider when concocting the perfect publicity campaign, but it is paramount to remember that in order to achieve the desire result, the mix of media must be just right.

Local & Community Print: The Base

This is the heart of any publicity campaign. Like an aged, smoky Rye, targeting print media publications forms the base of your PR cocktail—everything builds off of it. Articles placed in local and community magazines helps to establish visibility and lends to credibility in your particular field. When you are looking for the proper starting point, look no further than the printed page.

The diversity of readership and focus in the wide-range of print outlets allows for producing audience-specific content across a variety of industries, and positions you for the best chance of increased name-recognition and profit-margins. While the allure of a television or radio interview can seem enticing—*and they do have their place in the publicity mix*—

your information in local and community print publications offers permanence. A satellite outlet or emergency-broadcast message will not interrupt your expertise.

Broadcast: The Modifier

The purpose of a modifier in a drink, traditionally an additional liqueur such as Vermouth, is to enhance the impact of the base. That brings us to interviews and appearances on the broadcast medium, which works to augment your efforts in the area of print. The modifier will not make your campaign, but it will absolutely enrich it.

A targeted approach with radio and television, promoting events and engagements in a geographic-area, will provide a spike of PR activity that builds from your local and community print base. Your presence in print has brought your thoughts and ideas to your audience; your presence on their televisions and radios will put a face and voice to them.

Interviews & Op-Eds: The Flavor

The flavoring in an artisanal cocktail truly sets it apart from its traditional counterparts. Grenadine, tropical juices, ginger beer— ingenuity in flavors makes your beverage stand out; and the same is true for your publicity campaign.

Interviews that result in quotes in daily newspapers—local and national—and newsstand magazines bring your personality to the forefront. A controversial or distinct idea in the pages of publications with massive readerships puts your views on wide-display, and helps to establish you as a one-of-a-kind expert in your area.

Op-Eds take this a step further. They provide you with a forum to distinguish yourself from your colleagues, imparting a unique opinion or thought-process on your audience can make you a household name for your beliefs. Do not be afraid to push the envelope—professional mixologists take concerted risks to create a name for themselves.

Online Components: The Garnish

The garnish is the icing on the cocktail cake, if you will. You are finishing your creation with a flourish that doubles-down on your established base, modifier and flavors. The PR mix uses print outlets' online components as a garnish.

Since most—if not all—print media have an associated website, newsletter or blogging arm, many articles or interviews that appear in print will also be featured online. This achieves a dual-impact of your original piece, as it now exists on computer screens as well as in tangible print, which only helps to extend your reach.

With the advent of our social media society, articles online may garner even more mileage, as sharing pieces deemed particularly informative or valuable has become one of the cornerstones of Facebook and Twitter. You're only ever a few clicks and shares away from going viral.

There are few things as enjoyable as a finely-crafted cocktail. Mixologists behind bars across the globe are using their imaginative brains to create innovations-on-ice; using the classics as foundations to bring about something entirely original. The media mix for a publicity campaign should adhere to the same process: an emphasis on time-honored local and community print placements, a boost with broadcast media and heightened name-recognition with interviews and opposite-editorials. Top off your campaign with online features and exclusives and you have the mixture for the perfect publicity cocktail.

And you just may become the toast of the town.

About the Author

Russell Trahan is President of PR/PR, a boutique public relations agency specializing in positioning clients in front of their target audience in print and online. PR/PR represents experts of all kinds who are seeking national exposure for their business or organization. Russell and PR/

PR will raise your business' awareness in the eyes of your clients and customers. For more information, please visit **www.prpr.net**.

About the REAL Author:

 Carter Breazeale has been with PR/PR for more than five years. In addition to maintaining PR/PR's public relations blog, Carter has written pieces for the *Orlando Business Journal* and *AutoSuccess* magazine. He began his career in marketing/advertising at the national publication, *The Auto Trader*. From there, he has honed his client relationship skills as a Donor Advocate at Florida's Blood Centers. His degree in Psychology is from the University of Central Florida.

▶ SAMPLE ARTICLE FIVE

This is a great article on how to put your message into a format that speaks to your readers. The author is an attorney who specializes in intellectual property law. Rather than spout a bunch of boring legalese, we worked with him to find a common situation many businesses are concerned about. He told us about one of his most-often-asked questions. The article did very well, being placed in front of more than a dozen different industries and trades, showing how a very specific subject can still appeal to a general business audience.

Should I Copyright my Website?

By Andrew A. Gonzales, Esq.

The Internet makes it possible for businesses to reach millions of potential customers with a website. However, the Internet can be a source of liability for a company that is careless in publishing information.

If you have a blog, write articles, or manage an online magazine, chances are you have experienced—or will have—content stolen. The stolen content can be reposted on other blogs, article websites, and personal websites without proper attribution. Sometimes website content is copied in its entirety from your site to another website. There are also situations where your content is reposted with proper attribution, but without your permission.

The good news is that no matter how or why your content is used without your prior knowledge: there are measures you can take for such protection. There are even ways to prevent your content from being stolen in the first place.

How Do I Find Out If Content Has Been Stolen?

Set alerts which make it simple to keep an eye on your website content and potential piracy. Set alerts for both your domain name and business name so anytime they show up in the search engine, you receive notification.

Who Owns or Hosts the Site?

Contact the offending party directly to put them on notice to immediately remove infringing content. If this request falls on deaf ears, contact the online service provider [OSP]. OSPs are often more efficient when it comes to removing potentially infringing content than web owners.

The Digital Millennium Copyright Act [DMCA] is landmark legislation that updated U.S. Copyright Law to meet the demands of the digital age. You can also send a DMCA Takedown Notice to the OSP requesting that they remove or block the offending pages from the suspect website.

What is a Copyright?

Copyright is a form of protection given to authors of original works, including literary, dramatic, musical, artistic, and other intellectual works.

A copyright automatically comes into existence the moment an author fixes work in a tangible form. This protection gives the owner of a copyright several exclusive rights:

- to reproduce the work;
- to prepare derivative works (works that adapt the original work);
- to perform or display the work publicly;
- to distribute copies of the work to the public by sale, rent or lease.

Why Should I consider Copyright Registration?

You've probably noticed phrases like "All Rights Reserved" or "Copyright 2016", or perhaps the copyright symbol and a date at the bottom of a website. What does this mean? Do I need to copyright my website?

Registering a copyright with the United States Copyright Office is not mandatory. Copyright protection exists without registration; however, the "work" must be registered prior to filing an infringement case in court. In addition, the copyright owner will be eligible to receive statutory and actual damages as well as legal costs and attorneys' fees from a copyright infringer. Registration provides notice to the public that you own the work making it more difficult for someone to claim they unknowingly infringed upon your copyright. There is also added credibility registration brings to the work.

Should I Register my Website?

Copyright violation is illegal, but it can be difficult to prosecute offenders without copyright registration establishing a public record of ownership. If the content of your website is original(not a template), or if it includes an original work, it can be protected.

Website registration will generally be made to protect the textual, graphic and audio content of a site. All of these components should be submitted to obtain the broadest scope of legal protection.

Putting the Public on Notice

If a website contains copyrightable materials, a copyright notice should, at the very least, be placed on the site's home page. Although not required by law, it is not a bad idea to place notice on every page of the website. The circle © puts the world on notice that you claim a copyright in the work. The proper way to use the © is in connection with the year of first publication and the copyright owner's name (i.e.© 2016 Jane Doe or Copyright 2016 Jane Doe).

If you really want to make it clear that all aspects of your site are copyrighted, you may use a notice such as: All website design, text, graphics, selection and arrangement thereof, and software are the copyrighted works of Jane Doe © Copyright 2016.

Content theft on the Internet will always be a problem. Bear in mind that U.S. Copyright laws, cease and desist letters, careful monitoring, and all other actions can only get you so far. There is no 100% foolproof way to stop such action, but legal intervention may be warranted.

About the Author

Andrew A. Gonzalez, Esq. is an experienced attorney with over twenty five years in practice. He focuses his attention on business and intellectual property matters. He provides sophisticated services to commercial and individual clients who need to effectively compete in a business environment. For more information, please call 914 220-5474 or visit www.golawny.com.

▶ SAMPLE ARTICLE SIX

This article is a great example of the longevity of print and online placements. When it was initially pitched it received an above-average number of requests for the full text, as well as an average amount of placements over the next couple of months. In the following months, it continued to garner placements in print and online, even receiving a few placements over a year after the initial pitching process.

5 Qualities of a Lasting Leader

By Barry Banther

Leadership isn't just something you do, it's someone you become. But that requires a personal transformation, not just a personal agenda. Roger hadn't learned that lesson. During an interview for a new leadership position, the hiring manager asked why he switched jobs, and sometimes companies, every 3-5 years.

Roger blamed the employees who stopped growing and doubted ownership's commitment to the goal they asked him to reach. In other words, it had to be the environment because Roger was a "good" manager. Roger was half right—it was the environment. But he failed to recognize that he was responsible for creating that situation.

Lasting leaders, those who can weather economic downturns and even seismic market shifts in their employees or customers, are the ones who know how to assemble a diverse team and bring out their very best. If you're not building relationships that will last with your associates, even your financial success will be short-lived.

If we want to understand what really defines leaders then we have to start by looking at their followers. The old motivational tricks no longer work. Employees have become jaded from broken promises and failed dreams.

Today followers are drawn to leaders who show openness, invest time, listen, encourage and show appreciation for the strengths their employees bring to work. These are qualities that are developed intentionally over time but they pay dividends in both financial and personal performance for a lifetime.

Leaders who are held in the highest esteem for their success on both the bottom line and with the people they lead epitomize these 5 qualities. From their followers you will hear phrases like these: "he was always there for me," "I felt like she really listened," "he valued my opinion," and the result is employee engagement at the highest level. These qualities are gifts that a lasting leader is willing to give freely to the people they lead.

The Gift of Being Open to Others. Every leader claims to have an open-door policy. But it's not a leader's door that needs to be open— it's an open mind that matters! Openness encourages employee engagement, and that is fundamental to business success. The Gallup Organization's study of employee engagement in 7,939 business units in 36 different companies found that "employee engagement was positively associated with performance..."

The Gift of Investing Time in Others. Leaders are usually not solo inventors or lonely creative thinkers. They are called to assemble a team of people and enable them to be more productive together than any of them could be alone. Leaders can't create time, but when they invest their time to build profitable relationships with their employees they are multiplying the results they can achieve. Choosing to spend time with their employees daily is a leader's best return on time.

The Gift of Listening to Others. Trust between leaders and their associates is built upon a transparency that reflects a freedom to speak and be heard. Bad culture, where listening isn't valued, impacts business every day across America. It's been estimated that as much as 55% of a leader's work time is spent listening. But most leaders don't know how to do that. They confuse listening with hearing. When we are open to an employee's ideas and we invest the time to hear them then we are more apt to understand what they are saying and, sometimes more importantly, what they are not saying.

The Gift of Offering Encouragement to Others. Employees can work for hours without food or water. But they can't do quality work for more than a few minutes without hope; the hope that their work matters; the hope that they can get the job done and the hope that their effort will be appreciated by their boss. You have few chances as a leader to show respect for employees that is more potent than surprising them with words that show you believe they have what it takes to get the job done despite their current challenges.

The Gift of Expressing Appreciation for Others' Abilities. When a leader gives away genuine appreciation it is mirrored back in improved attitudes, stronger commitment and better performance. Study after study documents that employees do not feel appreciated. The gift of appreciation is not about altering your associates' opinion of the leader; it's about changing their opinion of themselves. When a leader helps employees believe in their unique strengths they build a work environment that—works! Lasting leaders know how to bring out the best in others.

You can be appointed someone's boss, but not their leader. Your followers ultimately determine your leadership. Had Roger developed these 5 gifts he might have still moved jobs every 3 -5 years but it wouldn't have been because he could no longer get results—it would be because he had developed a reputation for building a high performance team who followed his leadership even under tough conditions. That kind of leader is always in high demand.

About the Author

 Barry Banther is the founder and CEO of Banther Consulting. With decades of experience as a business leader and corporate executive, he has become a trusted advisor, leadership speaker and trainer for Fortune 100 companies like Pfizer and Rockwell as well as midsize to large family owned businesses across America. Barry's new book, "A Leader's Gift: How to Earn the Right to be Followed," will be released in April 2014. For more information, please visit www. barrybanther.com.

▶ **SAMPLE ARTICLE SEVEN**

This was a fun article to pitch, but we had to be careful when we did. The acronym used could be deemed a bit salacious to some, while to others it's a fun and attention-grabbing play on words. By taking the risk—but not being too risqué—we were able to place the article in more than a dozen print and online sources.

SOB or ESP: What's your Communication Style?

By Tracey C. "Tremendous" Jones

Texan: "Where are you from?"

Harvard Grad: "I come from a place where we do not end our sentences with prepositions."
Texan: "OK—where are you from, smart-aleck?"

We are rapidly losing the art of communication. The very trait which separates us from the animals is about to be our downfall, but fear not! There are ways we can rally and save humanity. First and foremost, ask yourself: Do I communicate to serve *myself* or do I communicate to serve *others*?

In other words, when you communicate, are you an SOB: (Self-Oriented Behavior) or do you use ESP: (Emotional, Spiritual, Personal)? In order to get to the heart of the issue, you have to get to the *heart*. Communication is not simply the external circuitry of words transmitted from your mouth to others' ears, but rather an internal reverberation of thoughts between your mind and your heart. Communication is simply the golden rule. It's part etiquette, part ethics, and part just being a decent human being. That means delineating boundaries for your emotional side so everyone can play in the sandbox nicely without getting into fights.

You can't expect people to see your point

of view if you can't see theirs. When we get squeezed what's inside comes out. All too often this takes the form of uncivil discourse. People are polarized by their tendency to see communication as a battle: somebody wins, somebody loses; too bad, so sad; in your face; suck it up, butter cup. It seems to be forgotten that for every action there is an equal and opposite reaction. And if you can't get comfortable floating in the fluidity of humanity, it's sunk.

Opinions are not a competitive sport. They are deeply held convictions. So here's a quick and easy way to assess if you are practicing great communication skills or if you are just being an SOB.

SOB: Self-Oriented Behavior. Let's face it: A lack of compassion is downright distasteful and has nothing to do with who or what is right and wrong. If you constantly feel the *need to seize* and to preach the "ministry of me" then you are an SOB communicator.

SOBs exhibit the following traits in their communication:

> Aggression
>
> Seeking sympathy
>
> Manipulation
>
> Clowning or mocking tone
>
> Competition
>
> Domination
>
> Labeling
>
> Bullying/cyberbullying

If you're an SOB, you view communication as a battlefield. Your level of indignation grants you the right to go from silence to thermonuclear in your content and tone. You have a hard time with dissenting points of view because you assume anyone who doesn't agree with you is a bigot. This type of behavior has been amplified by technology and mainstream media which grants unfiltered, unchecked, and ample coverage to an unending parade of poltroons. Winston Churchill said it best, "A fanatic is one who can't change his mind and won't change the subject."

Now let's look at the flip side of the coin: How can you best communicate with another in a way that affords the respect and civility that binds you to others in deeper and more knowledgeable ways? Here are the ways to win friends and influence people and ensure that you can talk to someone's heart, thus guaranteeing an open and honest dialogue sure to leave both parties enlightened and valued.

ESP: Emotional, Spiritual, Personal. It's like extrasensory perception on steroids. They say it ain't what you say, it's the way that you say it. Truer words were never spoken. The manner in which you connect is the most important factor in communication. If you do it well, the details are superfluous. Someone can completely disagree with everything you say, but still totally respect you as a person. The truth, no matter how hard it is to hear, should always have an element of love accompanying it. As the saying goes, a spoonful of sugar helps the medicine go down. The person who can accomplish this is a leader of unparalleled magnitude and a true uniter, not a divider.

ESPs exhibit the following traits in their communication:

> Individuality
>
> Respect
>
> The Golden Rule
>
> One-on-one
>
> Private
>
> Peace maker
>
> Acceptance
>
> Civility

The ESP communicator also understands that strongly held convictions do not necessarily classify someone as a "hater." They respect the other person's emotions and personal beliefs. Communication isn't some sort of Darwinian survival of the fittest. The ESP communicator firmly believes that we are not to trample one another out of existence with the butts of our heels and the slices of our tongues, but rather to be kind to one another, *especially* when during disagreements. Churchill had another great quote about this type of communicator, "Tact is the ability to tell someone to go to hell in such a way that they look forward to the trip."

Beautiful people see beauty; hateful people see hate. Someone once said, "Those who spend their time looking for the faults in others have no time to correct their own." Once you get serious about discussing and not just cussing, you'll take your communication to a new realm.

Be kind to humankind because it's all you've got.

About the Author

Tracey C. Jones, daughter of Charlie "Tremendous" Jones, is a US Air Force veteran, entrepreneur, speaker, and publisher. She speaks to audiences across the nation on leadership, accountability, business success, and other topics. Her latest book is "Beyond Tremendous: Raising the Bar on Life." To learn more visit www.TremendousTracey.com.

Acknowledgements

Writing a book is a team effort. Thank you to:

Carter Breazeale

Henry DeVries

Cathy Fyock

Pam Lontos

Patricia Fripp

Walt Grassl

Andrew A. Gonzales, Esq.

Barry Banther

Tracey C. "Tremendous" Jones

and

David Fernandez

About the Author

Russell Trahan is the owner and president of PR/PR Public Relations. PR/PR is a full-service boutique publicity agency specializing in professional speakers, consultants, and nonfiction authors. Since its founding in the late 1990s, PR/PR Public Relations has enjoyed a sterling track record of placing articles for 100 percent of their clients.

Russell joined the agency in 2005, after working for the Walt Disney Company, Clear Channel Radio, chambers of commerce, a downtown business association, and other nonprofit organizations. His educational background includes attending the Institute for Organizational Management at Stanford

University. When the founder retired in 2011, Russell purchased PR/PR Public Relations and continues its fine tradition of positioning clients in front of their target audiences through print media and online sources.

PR/PR's three main areas of service include placement of clients' articles in targeted trade and industry publications, securing interviews in newsstand magazines and daily newspapers, and developing a social-media-marketing messaging strategy for their clients. Whether they are well-established and want to stay current in their target markets' minds, or are emerging professionals who want the instant stamp of credibility that publicity brings, clients of PR/PR Public Relations achieve their publicity goals. PR/PR is Public Relations Producing Results.

54086419R00072

Made in the USA
San Bernardino, CA
06 October 2017